IMAGES
of America

AROUND
JACKSON

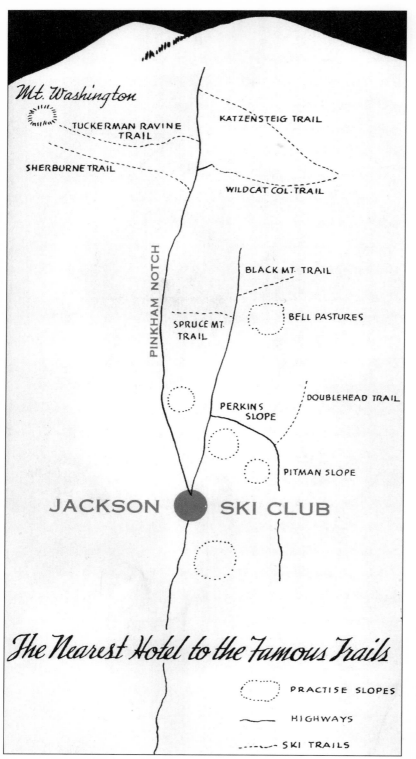

Mt. Washington

KATZENSTEIG TRAIL

TUCKERMAN RAVINE TRAIL

SHERBURNE TRAIL

WILDCAT COL. TRAIL

PINKHAM NOTCH

BLACK MT. TRAIL

BELL PASTURES

SPRUCE MT. TRAIL

DOUBLEHEAD TRAIL

PERKINS SLOPE

PITMAN SLOPE

JACKSON SKI CLUB

The Nearest Hotel to the Famous Trails

PRACTISE SLOPES

HIGHWAYS

SKI TRAILS

A ski map of the Jackson area from the Jackson Ski Club (an informal winter lodge of forty rooms) on Route 16, claiming to be "The Nearest Hotel to the Famous Trails."

IMAGES
of America

AROUND
JACKSON

By
Richard N. Johnson

ARCADIA

First published 1995
Copyright © Richard N. Johnson, 1995

ISBN 0-7524-0223-4

Published by Arcadia Publishing,
an imprint of the Chalford Publishing Corporation
One Washington Center, Dover, New Hampshire 03820
Printed in Great Britain

Library of Congress Cataloging-in-Publication Data applied for

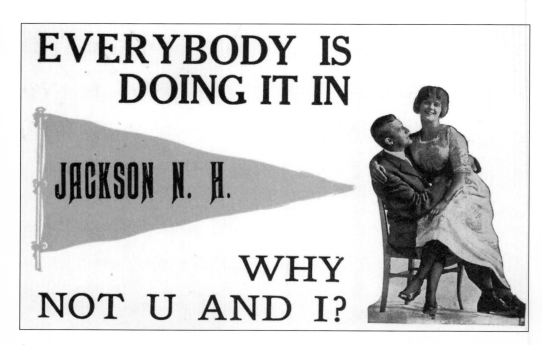

Contents

In honor of my mother, Herta Fruchtenicht Buske,
in memory of my father, Carl Henry Johnson,
and with respect to the founding families and their descendants of
the village of Jackson, New Hampshire,
I dedicate this book.

Introduction

Around Jackson is a photographic journey over the past one hundred years. In collecting over seven hundred postcards of Jackson, I have attempted to avoid all "chromes," which represent the 1960s to the present. The popularity of Jackson has never failed to amaze me, and I continue to find new cards and photographs of Jackson and the surrounding area.

In the past eight years, I have called Jackson my home, and now I proudly submit this work as another part of its recorded history. I am truly amazed that, to date, there has not been a written volume of the entire history of New Madbury, Adams, and Jackson—a future endeavor, perhaps.

I am certain that many of you will find fond memories of yesterday and your youth in these pages. Many of you will wish you had the opportunity to have lived here in the late 1800s and early 1900s. Through these photographs, you have the opportunity to let your imagination return you to an earlier Jackson, not a better or more beautiful one, just an earlier one.

Jackson, New Hampshire, is truly "A spot of Gold in the White Mountains," as the Jackson Chamber of Commerce claimed in their promotional material for a number of years. It offers so much! The quality of life offered here is unchallengeable, the beauty of the area breath-taking and pristine, and the people are the family you always wished for. Hopefully, these elements will surface as you enjoy this book.

I wish to thank the following Jacksonites who took the time to assist me, either through research, the use of their photographs, or the encouragement that they offered. My thanks to Ed March, Rodney Charles, Charlotte Haskell, Robin Crocker, Marty and Pam Sweeney, Kevin Martin, Bob Bowman, Marty Sage Gilman, Barbara Lubao, Carl Slack, and Fritz Koeppel.

With warmest memories, I thank Meg Garland who encouraged me, continuously supported me in my collection of Jackson postcards, and who shared many of her thoughts and memories. Her book *Yesterdays* has been a valuable source of Jackson history and hopefully will be reprinted in the not too distant future.

Richard N. Johnson

One

White Mountain Highway

White Mountain Highway, now referred to as Route 16, once passed through the village itself, but now bypasses a brief distance to the west. This photograph was taken on April 1 and indicates the more severe weather often experienced in the past.

This path was most likely the same path traveled by Benjamin Copp when he first settled in 1778. First known as Gilman's Grant, then New Madbury and later Adams, it became Jackson on July 4, 1829.

The Goodrich Falls Tourist Camp, just south of Jackson, boasted overnight cabins ($1 per person), tenting space ($1 per car), a restaurant, mineral spring, flush closets, shower baths, swimming pool, and community room.

Here we view the majestic site of the Goodrich Falls on the Ellis River, just south of the village. The Goodrich Falls Covered Bridge, built in 1866 and replaced in 1938, spanned the river just above the hydro-electric plant that continues in operation today.

A favorite swimming hole for local residents and visitors, the cold clear waters of the Ellis River at the base of the Goodrich Falls made the trek of over one hundred steps worthwhile on a warm summer day.

The area above the dam was also popular as a swimming area. This photograph was taken during the final days of the covered bridge before it was replaced by a then modern structure.

Streeter's Cottages and Cabins, where many local residents and visitors enjoyed home cooking at Kelly's Restaurant. Streeter's is currently the location of many of the original cabins and offices of the Nordic Village.

One of the Streeter's cottages that sits near the creek that flows from across the White Mountain Highway into the Ellis River. These cabins and cottages were very popular in the late 1940s.

If you called Jackson #54, you could soon be on your way to spending a retreat vacation at Kern's Court, fly fishing in the Ellis River. The cabins were modern, clean, convenient, and right on the water.

The telephone number has become EVergreen 3–4242 in this photograph (the same number it has today), and the automobiles are from the 1950s, but the fishing, convenience, and cleanliness remain the same today.

The Iron Mountain House was originally built in 1861 by James M. Meserve. It was rebuilt and opened in 1885 by J.M. Meserve and son after a fire destroyed the original in 1877. The hotel opened in early June and operated until late October, but special arrangements could be made for winter guests from December through March.

The grandeur of 1905 is evident in this photograph, as the Willard family of Franklin, Massachusetts, prepares to depart the Iron Mountain House for a day of adventure in the White Mountains.

The Iron Mountain House, sitting at the base of the mountain for which it is named, is at the southern end of the entrance to the village. The establishment had accommodations for over one hundred guests, with steam heat, the best of modern plumbing, electricity, and fresh produce from its own farm.

An artist's drawing from one of the old brochures of the Iron Mountain House illustrating Meserve Hall (which remains today retaining the Iron Mountain House name) and the main building, connected by broad verandas awaiting guests to arrive by rail from the Glen station.

One of the original snowmobiles as it carries winter revelers past the tennis courts of the Iron Mountain House out for a winter adventure in the early 1900s.

The host site of the American Lawn Tennis tournaments in August 1913. The event brought tennis greats from throughout the states to the Iron Mountain House courts, situated on the banks of the Ellis River. Two of the original lawn tennis courts were reactivated in the late 1930s but closed again with the onset of World War II.

The Jackson Covered Bridge, known as the Honeymoon Bridge, was built by Charles A. Broughton and his son Frank in 1876. It is of Paddleford truss design and is 121 feet and 1 inch long, with a clear span of 103 feet. The overall width is 26 feet and 5 inches, with a roadway width of 16 feet and a maximum clearance of 12 feet 3 inches. It spans the Ellis River and has a sidewalk on the upstream side. The structure was built with exposed sides.

Decorated for the holidays, the Honeymoon Bridge welcomes home residents and guests to the village. The sidewalk was added in 1930, and in 1965 the approach from Route 16 was rebuilt to improve visibility and to provide parking. The bridge has become one of the most photographed memories of one's visit to Jackson.

This Shorey Studio photograph of the Jackson Covered Bridge beckons tourists with "Hotels, Post Office, Stores, Gas Stations"—what more could you ask for?

A seldom seen view of the Honeymoon Bridge looking upsteam. Note the Paddleford truss as it arches upward. The trusses were originally more exposed when first constructed in the late 1870s. This bridge is eligible for listing on the National Register of Historic Places and has been initially approved by the NH Historical Society for its entrance to that listing.

Through the portals of the Jackson Covered Bridge come the famous Clydesdale horses taking part in the Jackson Bicentennial celebration in 1978. New Hampshire Covered Bridge #51 must have neared its 6-ton limit on that afternoon.

A view of the village of Jackson from Green Hill. Many of the buildings are part of the Wentworth Hall complex. The large building at the lower left is the Glen Ellis House. The original White Mountain Highway was just east of the one today. The Jackson Community Church steeple is just visible to the lower right, and take special note of all the cleared farming land towards Doublehead in the background of the photograph.

"The bridge is very near the hotel and every time a team or auto goes over it you would think it was thundering . . ." wrote Inzie Netzeba on this postcard from August 11, 1915, of the old Ellis River Bridge. The new bridge when constructed was placed only a few hundred feet upstream.

Just up the road from that "thundering" bridge sat the Glen Ellis House originally built by Nicholas T. Stillings in 1876 on the direct road to Pinkham Notch. The Thompson House remains today on the left side of the road across from the Glen Ellis House.

After the death of Nicholas T. Skillings, the Glen Ellis House was operated by his daughter, Mrs. S.S. Thompson. She was the mother of Harry Thompson, a lawyer, who ran the stage coach line from Jackson to the top of Mount Washington.

Mirror Lake, also known as Mill Pond, supplied many of the 2-by-2-by-3 blocks of ice for the major inns and resorts in the late 1800s prior to the arrival of refrigeration. It was also the site of a clothes pin factory, a dowel factory, and a sawmill over the early years.

Alice and Andrew Harriman at their farm along the Glen Ellis River off the White Mountain Highway. Mr. Harriman, a carpenter, built the original schoolhouse in Jackson and rebuilt the Jackson Town Hall after its fire in 1895. Many of the older homes in Jackson were built by Mr. Harriman.

The Harriman farm, home of Alice and Andrew Harriman and their ten children, provided living quarters for many employees of the inns and resorts of Jackson. The farm is now the location of the Ellis River House.

The Oak Lee Ski Lodge and Barracks has served guests to the village since the late 1800s. Once known as Maple Cottage, its owners have included Dressers, Meserves, Goodmans, and Stilpens. The Mulkerns purchased the Oak Lee in the early 1950s and now operate it as the Shannon Door Pub.

The Oak Lee Ski Barracks await their tired guests after a long day of adventurous skiing in Tuckerman's Ravine and the rest of the White Mountain ski areas. The Oak Lee also lays claim to fame for being the bar scene in the Hollywood production of the *Return of the Secaucus Seven*, a motion picture from the 1960s.

Abbott's Cottage was a comfortable farm house with hot and cold running water, baths and comfortable beds, and home cooking of excellent quality, all at reasonable rates. From 1934 to the late 1970s the family of Ida Meserve Abbott hosted many famous skiers who visited the area.

The original roadside art gallery of one of Jackson's resident artists, David C. Baker. Mr. Baker's paintings are recognized far and wide and are a valued and much sought after prize for both visitors and residents alike.

The Ellis River Cabins and Restaurant, just four miles north of the village, offered guests cabins along the Ellis River and White Mountain Highway. The restaurant is a well-remembered dining place of Jackson residents.

The interior of the Ellis River Restaurant, complete with spinning wheel and local antiques, served steaks, chops, salads, home-baked beans, sandwiches, waffles, and "good coffee."

The Dana Place Inn, originally the site of the Ontwin Dana Farm (1874). In the 1890s a larger house was built to accommodate summer visitors; known as the Fern Cliff Farm, it soon became a stopover for the stage coaches from the top of Mount Washington. After a number of private owners, Stanley Davidson, a Boston architect, once again opened the inn to travelers in 1946.

The Glen Ellis Falls, originally known as "Pitcher Falls," was renamed in 1852 by Henry Shepley of Portland, Maine. It is some 70 feet high, easily accessible to visitors by a footpath, and continues to attract people to its beautiful and majestic views.

The Crystal Cascade is associated with an Indian legend. A chief's daughter wished to wed a brave from another tribe; after a competition of sorts, her lover, who lost, escaped with her swiftly into the nearby woods. After finding it impossible to escape the pursuit, the two lovers jumped hand in hand into the Cascade. The legend states that, even to this day, their forms can be seen amid the glittering mist.

The Painted Trail of Tuckerman's Ravine is seldom seen without snow covering its lack of vegetation. Tuckerman's Ravine was named in honor of Dr. Edward Tuckerman (Amherst College) who first visited the area in 1837. He was responsible for characterizing the vegetation into four distinct categories: the Alpine zone, the sub-Alpine zone, the upper forest, and the lower forest.

The main headwall of Tuckerman's Ravine looms before you. It's 1939, and to this day the record of 6 minutes 29 seconds from the top of the headwall to Pinkham's Notch has never been broken. The Inferno Ski Race, once a tradition as part of the rites of spring, has been long discontinued, but the masses still flock to Tuckerman's every spring long after snow has disappeared from the rest of the northeast.

An old photograph of a family outing in the late 1800s as they pass near the entrance to the Mount Washington Carriage Road to the summit of Mount Washington. The charter was granted for the construction of the road in 1853 and it was completed in 1861.

The Glen House and Stables at the base of the Mount Washington Carriage (Auto) Road eventually had rooms for two hundred guests. In the late 1800s visitors would ascend Mount Washington via the Cog Railway and descend via the Carriage Road, resting overnight at the Glen House.

In 1861, if you traveled the road on foot it only cost 2¢ a mile; it was 3¢ for a horse and rider, and 5¢ for a horse and carriage. A Stanley Steamer was the first automobile to ascend the auto road (1899), and in the years to follow the road has hosted many races to the summit. Today, you can race by car, bike, or on foot during the summer months (the footrace is so popular, runners have to be chosen by lottery).

The Mount Washington Auto Road is placed almost exactly today as it was planned in the early 1850s. The road is 8 miles long with an average grade of 12 percent and a maximum grade of 26 percent, and was to be constructed at a cost of $8,000 per mile. Construction began in 1854 with funds for the project running out in 1857 just above the Halfway House.

In 1859 a new corporation, with the financial support of David Pingree, was formed after receiving the right for the roadway and right of way. The road was completed in 1861. The owner of the Glen House, Joseph Thompson, drove the first vehicle to the summit, that being a one-horse buckboard, before the road was officially completed.

In 1880, a drunken driver of a four-horse mountain wagon died along with one of his passengers after overturning on the road. In 1984, another fatality was recorded when the brakes on a vehicle failed on the decent of the mountain. It has become a very common sight throughout the country to see the "This car climbed Mount Washington" bumper stickers.

Along the Peabody River flowing from Mount Washington in the distance. This section of the White Mountain Highway travels north to the cities of Gorham and Berlin on the other side of Pinkham Notch.

Two
The Village Loop

Just over the Jackson Covered Bridge, on the left, you will see "The Blue Spruces" as it was known for a brief period when the Dearborns owned the home. Now a private residence belonging to Flossie Gile, it was once owned by Howard Gray, a member of the Gray's Inn family. To the right of the home remains the Gray's Inn garage where the horses and vehicles of guests were kept.

The Robinwood Inn, also known as the Checkerberry Inn and the Nestlenook Inn, is said to be part of the oldest building in Jackson. Part of this building was once a section of the old Wiggleworth farm on Thorn Hill Road. It was moved here by Fred and Josephine Dinsmore in 1900 and became their home. The first guests arrived in 1906, and it then became the Nestlenook Inn.

In 1945, Nestlenook Inn became the Checkerberry Inn when the Freemans purchased it. It has since been owned by the Bradys, the Volckmans, the Doerflers, and the Burns, under the names of Robinwood Inn and Nestlenook Farm. It has been completely refurbished in the last few years and has been returned to a Victorian era lodging place.

The toboggan slide at Gray's Inn. In the 1920s, Gray's Inn opened part-time during the winter months for groups who wished to snowshoe and toboggan in the village.

Gray's Inn, the second one, was built on the same location as the original Sunset Hill House which opened in 1885. The complex consisted of Woodbury Hall, Merrill Cottage, a casino, a studio, and a laundry house. The Inn's four-month summer season ran from June 15 to October 15, with guests arriving by train from Massachusetts, Connecticut, Rhode Island, and New York.

Note the difference in construction of this Gray's Inn, also destroyed by fire, from the previous photograph. The guests of Gray's Inn, usually families, came for the summer and were treated to entertainment in the form of classical concerts, dancing, visiting choirs, and traveling magicians. In the 1920s the Inn added a 9-hole golf course, located in Glen, 2 miles south on the White Mountain Highway.

Again, note the different architecture of this Gray's Inn building—the central tower is the most obvious change. The last of four fires struck a vacant boarded up fire hazard on July 14, 1983, ending an era of refinement and fond memories in less than an hour.

By 1 pm, a half hour after Sherrill Kelly saw smoke at the back of the Gray's Inn property, the entire building was engulfed in flames. Jackson Fire Chief Willis Kelly estimated temperatures exceeded 1,000 degrees as varnish dripped off the porch of the Village House, across the street. As the fire department pumped 4,000 gallons per minute of water, they knew there was nothing they could do to save the sixty-six-year-old structure.

Within an hour, all that was left of Gray's Inn were charred remains and the foundation of a grand old building. Although arson was suspected, no charges have ever been filed regarding the responsibility of the fire. In 1988, the residents of Jackson voted to purchase the 33-acre parcel, owned by the Loew family of Boston, for one million dollars.

A postcard by George Slade, a popular Jackson photographer, captures the joy and excitement of these residents and visitors as they participate in the then favorite winter sports of tobogganing and snowshoeing in the village of Jackson. Many of the local inns made special arrangements for the winter visitors to enjoy the vast amounts of natural snow.

The Hawthorne Inn, originally the Towle Farm, was built by Jonathan Meserve in the mid-1800s. The Inn boasted its own cows, vegetable gardens, and the same cook, Iva Nute, for over two decades. Its annex building, clay tennis courts, and ideal location attracted many repeat vacationers.

"Where skiers gather" was well-known as the motto of the Hawthorne Inn complex in the 1930s. Local ski instructor Arthur Doucette could often be found gathered around a table with other skiers and winter visitors. The Inn and annex were usually packed with skiers, who often filled the halls with sleeping bags on weekends and during vacations. It burned down in 1973.

The Hawthorne Inn, now the Village House, is a favorite of the author, and his small antique shop specializing in Jackson and White Mountain postcards and photo memorabilia can be seen at the far left of this photograph.

A photograph of Main Street, Jackson Village, as it intersects with Thorn Hill Road, which travels over Thorn Hill to the village of Intervale. Black Mountain can be seen in the distance.

The Thorn Hill Lodge, at the base of Thorn Hill Road, was owned by Tom and Ruth Darville, who ran it as a boarding house for summer and winter guests. Note the bicycle for rent sign near the lodging sign.

This is a photograph of downtown Jackson with the new Jack Frost Shop on the left. The Mobil gas station, the Jackson Grammar School, and the Jackson Falls House can be seen in the background.

Bessie's, owned and operated by Bessie Rogers, was the local outlet for Maple Grove postcards, maple candies, maple sugar and syrup, white birch beer, Blanchard's ice cream, and Balsam pillows. Helen's Beauty Shop was located in the rear of the building.

Saks Fifth Avenue and Carroll Reed Shops in Jackson? Both shops were located in the Wildcat
Inn and Tavern block, along with the Western Union and the Eastern Slope Ski School. The
school was the American branch of the Hannes Schneider Ski School of St. Anton Am Alberg,
Austria, and had Benno Rybizka as an instructor.

Carroll Reed patiently awaits another group of students for the Eastern Slope Ski School. Lessons today are given at Black Mountain behind Whitneys' in Jackson.

A winter view of Main Street with the skis having been added to the Thorn Mountain Lodge. The Lodge later became the S-Kimos, a private ski club with members from Massachusetts and Rhode Island.

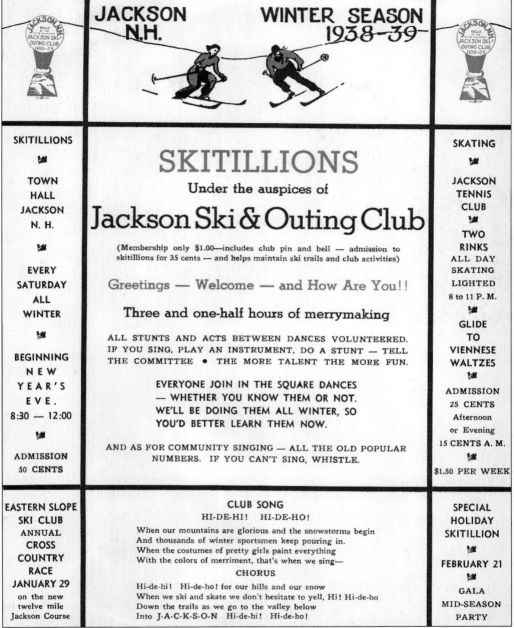

JACKSON N.H.

WINTER SEASON 1938-39

SKITILLIONS

🔔

TOWN HALL
JACKSON N. H.

🔔

EVERY SATURDAY ALL WINTER

🔔

BEGINNING NEW YEAR'S EVE.
8:30 — 12:00

🔔

ADMISSION 50 CENTS

SKITILLIONS

Under the auspices of

Jackson Ski & Outing Club

(Membership only $1.00—includes club pin and bell — admission to skitillions for 35 cents — and helps maintain ski trails and club activities)

Greetings — Welcome — and How Are You!!

Three and one-half hours of merrymaking

ALL STUNTS AND ACTS BETWEEN DANCES VOLUNTEERED. IF YOU SING, PLAY AN INSTRUMENT, DO A STUNT — TELL THE COMMITTEE • THE MORE TALENT THE MORE FUN.

EVERYONE JOIN IN THE SQUARE DANCES — WHETHER YOU KNOW THEM OR NOT. WE'LL BE DOING THEM ALL WINTER, SO YOU'D BETTER LEARN THEM NOW.

AND AS FOR COMMUNITY SINGING — ALL THE OLD POPULAR NUMBERS. IF YOU CAN'T SING, WHISTLE.

SKATING

🔔

JACKSON TENNIS CLUB

🔔

TWO RINKS
ALL DAY SKATING
LIGHTED
8 to 11 P. M.

🔔

GLIDE TO VIENNESE WALTZES

🔔

ADMISSION
25 CENTS
Afternoon
or Evening
15 CENTS A. M.

🔔

$1.50 PER WEEK

EASTERN SLOPE SKI CLUB ANNUAL CROSS COUNTRY RACE
JANUARY 29
on the new twelve mile Jackson Course

CLUB SONG
HI-DE-HI!   HI-DE-HO!

When our mountains are glorious and the snowstorms begin
And thousands of winter sportsmen keep pouring in.
When the costumes of pretty girls paint everything
With the colors of merriment, that's when we sing—

CHORUS

Hi-de-hi! Hi-de-ho! for our hills and our snow
When we ski and skate we don't hesitate to yell, Hi! Hi-de-ho
Down the trails as we go to the valley below
Into J-A-C-K-S-O-N Hi-de-hi! Hi-de-ho!

SPECIAL HOLIDAY SKITILLION

🔔

FEBRUARY 21

🔔

GALA MID-SEASON PARTY

This is a copy of the flier announcing the Jackson Ski & Outing Club Skitillion events for the 1938–39 winter season. This winter there were to be dances at the Town Hall every Saturday beginning on New Years Eve, skating at the Jackson Tennis Club's two rinks, the Eastern Slope Ski Club annual cross country race, and the special Holiday Skitillion gala mid-season party.

The White Rabbit Gift Shop, Western Union, and another gift shop (run by A.E. Phinney, a local photographer) were housed in what is today the Wildcat Inn & Tavern block.

The ingenuity of man is illustrated in this photograph, as the haying is completed with a home-made tractor in the present day Jackson village park. The newly constructed Jack Frost Shop, Jackson Grammar School, and Jackson Falls House can be seen in the background.

A lone horse feeds where the current Jack Frost Shop parking lot is located. Note the Jackson Public Library, Jackson Community Church, and the Wentworth Hall on the far side of the Wildcat River.

This wood lot, right in downtown Jackson, overlooks Weber's Drug Store and the Mobil gas station. The Jackson Grammar School can be seen on the right and the Wentworth Hall is on the far left.

Weber's Drug Store, now Yesterday's Restaurant, served village residents and visitors for many years as Fred Weber carefully weighed out those apothecary mixtures.

A view of Main Street from the Stone Bridge, directly in front of the Wentworth Hall. This photograph was taken prior to the construction of the Jack Frost Shop.

This load of hay is headed for the Jackson Falls House barn located directly behind the Jackson Grammar School. There were once six schools serving the students in the village, with the first school having been built in 1806. The one-story building was located on the same site as this current school.

Ed March is having a difficult time moving the snow from his driveway behind Weber's Drug Store. Many of the older residents claim winters are no longer as severe as they previously experienced.

This page is made up of personal calling cards popular in the late 1800s and early 1900s. Many of these cards were once owned by well-known families in Jackson, such as the Meserves, Fernalds, Pinkhams, Hayes, and Hacketts. They often carried special messages to celebrate holidays and other events.

Treasurer's Report.

Balance in treasury Feb. 15, 1905,	$ 290 23
Rec'd of C. S. Meserve, overdrawn order,	1 32
Collector of 1902, taxes,	3 48
" 1903,	6 22
" 1904,	590 02
" 1905,	4,558 44
Land sales 1902-03,	42 40
License commission,	20 58
N. I. Trickey, dog license,	94 40
Billiard and pool license,	27 25
Use of hearse,	2 00
Selectmen, for cement,	2 00
" hired money,	2,200 00
County, for poor,	78 00
State, for bounties,	18 00
" savings bank tax,	185 44
" literary fund,	60 50
N. I. Trickey, use of town house,	47 00
	———— $8,227 28
Paid out by orders,	8,184 01
	————
Balance in treasury,	$ 43 27

WILLIAM W. TRICKEY,
Town Treasurer.

This is a copy of the Treasurer's Report by William W. Trickey, taken from the Annual Report of the Town of Jackson for the fiscal year ending February 15, 1906.

VITAL STATISTICS.

To the Selectmen :--In compliance with an act of the legislature passed June Session, 1887, requiring clerks of towns and cities to furnish a transcript of the record of births, marriages, and deaths to the municipal officers for publication in the Annual Report, I hereby submit the following :

BIRTHS REGISTERED IN THE TOWN OF JACKSON, N. H., FOR THE YEAR ENDING DECEMBER 31, 1905.

Date.	Name of the Child (if any)	Male or Female	Living or Stillborn	No. of child, 1st,	Color.	Name of Father.	Maiden Name of Mother.	Color of Parents.	Residence of Parents.	Occupation of Father.	Birthplace of Father.	Birthplace of Mother.
May 11		Female	Living	5	White	Osborn F Fernald	Elizabeth Meserve	White	Jackson	Farmer	Jackson	Fryeburg Me
30		"	"	3		Fred M Dinsmore	Josie A Mansfield		"	"	"	"
Sept 7		Male	"	2		Edwin J Gile	Verpie F Hayes		"	Lumberman	Stowe Me	Jackson
8		"	"	11		Wallace I Hayes	Etta D Abbott		"	Farmer	Jackson	"
Oct 5		Female	"	1		Dana Haley	Blanche E Hayes		"	Laborer	Fryeburg Me	"
29		Male	"	3		Jason C Gile	Eva D Hatch		"	Farmer	Stowe Me	Effingham
Nov 9		Female	"	5		Geo L Howard	Clara A Davis		"	"	Dover Mass	Jackson
21		Male	"	1		Dean W Davis	Eva L Magner		"	"	Jackson	Leeds Me
27		"	"	3		Winthrop Dearborn	Cora L Learred		"	Laborer	"	Guildhall Vt
29		Female	"	6		Asa A Abbott	Marantha F Grant		"	"	"	Jackson
10		"	"	1		Irving H Abbott	Mattie M Charles		"	"	"	Fryeburg Me

The births registered in the Town of Jackson for the year ending December 31, 1905, as documented by N.I. Trickey, the town clerk. They were listed under the Vital Statistic section of the Annual Report.

Town Warrant

THE STATE OF NEW HAMPSHIRE

To the Inhabitants of the Town of Jackson, in the County Carroll in said State qualified to vote in town affairs:

You are hereby notified to meet at the Town House in said Jackson, on Tuesday, the fourteenth day of March next, at nine of the clock in the forenoon to act upon the following subjects:

1. To choose all necessary Town Officers for the ensuing year.

2. To raise and appropriate such amount of money as may be necessary to defray town charges for the ensuing year.

3. To see what amount of money the town will vote to raise and appropriate for highways and bridges.

4. To see if the town will vote to raise and appropriate the sum of $500 for State Aid Maintenance of Highways.

5. To see if the town will vote to raise and appropriate the sum of $1700 for Trunk Line Maintenance of Highways.

6. To see if the town will vote to raise and appropriate the sum of $949.50 for State Aid Construction of Highways

7. To see what amount of money the town will vote to raise and appropriate for the maintenance of the cemetery.

8. To see if the town will vote to recommend abolishing the Special District.

9. To see if the town will vote to guarantee Radcliffe Chautauqua $500, transportation from and to Glen, site for tent, labor erecting tent and taking down tent, in return for all receipts for two full days entertainment, it being agreed Chautauqua meetings be held in August upon dates not conflicting with North Conway Chautauqua.

ARTHUR P. GALE,
DEAN W. DAVIS,
WALTER J. WENTWORTH.
Selectmen of Jackson.

This was the Town Warrant to be acted upon on March 14, 1923. Take special note of Article 9, requesting the sum of $500 to be appropriated for a Chautauqua meeting in Glen. The Town of Jackson obviously was hoping to use these educational seminars to bring added income to their treasury.

REPORT of THE SUPERINTENDENT of SCHOOLS

To the School Board and Citizens of Jackson
Special District:

I have the honor to present my Annual Report of the condition and work of your schools. There are 53 pupils registered in the schools with two teachers. The pupils are doing good work and are well supplied with books and supplies. The Schoolhouse is in urgent need of alteration. The general condition of the house is bad when compared with schoolhouses in other parts of the state. The lighting, heating, ventilation and the toilets are bad and this should be taken into consideration at your District Meeting. It becomes my duty under the law to call your attention to the condition of your schoolhouse and to the fact that it is a menace to the health of your children. I suggest that an expert on schoolhouse construction be employed to advise what should be done to make your school safe for your children.

Hoping that more of the citizens who have children in school will take the trouble to visit the school and thus know at first hand the conditions surrounding the children. A visit will also show your sympathy with the teachers and pupils and thus encourage better work in the school.

Respectfully yours,
L. M. FELCH

L.M. Felch, superintendent of schools, isn't too pleased with the condition of the school. He states "the lighting, heating, ventilation and toilets are bad . . ." and ". . . that is a menace to your children."

Alice P. Trickey, daughter of General George P. Meserve, and her husband, Joseph B. Trickey, built and operated the Jackson Falls House.

An outing of guests and family members of the Jackson Falls House enjoying a summer afternoon exploring the White Mountains.

The beautifully decorated coach of the Jackson Falls House and its team of six, with employees and family members, compete in a coaching parade in Intervale, New Hampshire, in 1894. The

Jackson Falls House, as well as other hotels in the village, would send its coach to Glen and Intervale to pick up guests arriving at the rail stations.

The Jackson Falls House was built in 1858 by the Joseph B. Trickey family. It was the first and only hotel in Jackson for many years. The barn at the far right is the only remaining building of this grand hotel.

George P. Trickey, the bachelor of the family, is on the left in this photograph of guests enjoying a "picturesque moment" on the porch of the original Jackson Falls House.

By 1885, the Jackson Falls House was in dire need of additional room because of increased business. In November 1885, the entire house was raised and a first floor with high ceilings was added under the original structure. Soon an annex was built, and ells were added to the annex.

The Jackson Falls House as it looked prior to its sale to Daniel R. Blanchard in 1946. Note the balconies where the doors were located prior to the building being raised.

The Iron Bridge crossed the Wildcat River directly in front of the Jackson Town Hall and came out in front of the Wentworth Hall. The Crow's Nest, on the left, was a popular spot to relax and view the river and Jackson Falls.

These three ladies in Victorian attire are out for a stroll between the Wentworth Hall and the Jackson Falls House.

This was Howard Robinson's store, the Wigwam, which sold fresh meats, groceries, dry goods, and just about everything else that tourists and residents of the village required. The second and third floors were used for family quarters and housed employees from various inns in the village.

The Wentworth Hall was originally known as the Thorn Mountain House, having been built by Joshua Trickey in 1869. His daughter married Marshall Wentworth, and over the years they added Arden Cottage, Wentworth Hall, Thornycroft, Wildwood Cottage, Glen-Thorne, Elmwood, and many more buildings. The complex was self-sustaining and could accommodate over four hundred guests and employees. In the 1920s, when Wentworth Hall was in its prime, it was owned by Nathan Amster, a railroad tycoon from New York.

We will probably never know why Oscar Meserve never received his check for $85 on October 10, 1899. It was drawn on the First National Bank of Portland, Maine.

The Wentworth Hall management, realizing the value of sanitary milk, built the most perfect pasteurizing plant in America. Guests were served fresh butter, and milk and cream in individually sealed bottles (or so this postcard by Walter Dole claims).

General Marshall Wentworth was extremely popular and well-liked by the guests, employees, and local residents. Every year he would host an annual party, and sent printed invitations to every child in Jackson.

The Wildwood Cottage and the Jackson Public Library were moved in the late 1930s to make room for the construction of the new Stone Bridge over the Wildcat River. The library was eventually moved next to the Jackson Community Church where it remains today.

This photograph of the Stone Bridge, taken from the Wentworth Hall, looks toward the village with Thorn Mountain in the background, majestically clouded with early morning haze.

John K. Porter of Boston, Massachusetts, who was a guest in 1879 at the Thorn Mountain House (later to become the Wentworth Hall), suggested a "Free Public Library for the Town of Jackson, NH." Stone work began on the library in October 1900 and the building was opened to the public on August 1, 1901.

Church.
Jackson, N. H.
Sept. 1907.

The first church in Jackson was the Free-Will Baptist Church, founded in 1803. The church was located at the triangle where Black Mountain and Wilson Roads intersect. On February 28, 1846, a group split from the church and formed the Protestant Chapel Association. In order to afford the building of the church pictured here (now named the Jackson Community Church), the members individually purchased their pews.

This view, from the present golf course, illustrates just how mammoth a complex the Wentworth Hall was. The thirty-nine buildings included an electric plant, a farm, greenhouses, a laundry, a dairy and pasteurization plant, a blacksmith shop, a printers shop, a telegraph office, a gift boutique, a casino, a garage with mechanics, a barber shop and beauty parlor, three dining rooms, and a 6-hole golf course (later enlarged to 18 holes).

The seventh hole of the Wentworth Golf Course as par is about to be made on a delightful summer afternoon.

The Wentworth Golf Course will celebrate its 100th anniversary this year, as it was the first in the village to entice vacationing golfers in 1895. The Eagle Mountain House Golf Course of 6 holes followed in 1900 and Gray's Inn opened their course, 2 miles south in Glen, in the 1920s. The Spruce Mountain Lodge also had a short 5-hole course on Carter Notch Road.

The Wildcat Valley Country Store returned people to yesteryear and served visitors and residents penny candy, dry goods, and many other items found only in old country stores. The building was once a blacksmith shop owned and operated by the father of Rodney Charles, a longtime Jackson resident.

This photograph shows the old-time penny candy section with jars of tempting confectionaries and displays of articles common to the first settlers of the area. The Wildcat Valley Country Store maintained a catalogue business for a number of years.

The road into the village curved at a much sharper degree passing in front of the Thompson residence (now the Thompson House Eatery) before intersecting with the White Mountain Highway. The Glen Ellis House was located directly beyond that on the way into "Jackson City."

This road leads to the Wildcat River, and prior to 1865, the center of the village was on this side of the river, boasting a clothes pin factory, dowel factory, sawmill, post office, church, blacksmith shop, general store, and grist mill.

Three

Thorn Mountain
and Tyrol

The Inn at Jackson was originally built in 1902 as a private home for the Baldwin family of New York (of piano fame). It became Gray Manor in 1922 and was operated as a summer inn until 1935. Owners after the Grays included the Ropes, Greens, Gaults, Beals, Landrys, and Ferrys. During this period it acquired the name "Jackson Lodge." For the past ten years it has served as the Inn at Jackson.

The Inn at Thorn Hill, another home designed by Sanford White, was originally operated as a boarding house under the name of Brookmead. When the Pitmans sold the home to Howard Moody in 1932, it became known as Moody Cottages. In 1974 the Darvilles changed the name to the Thorn Hill Lodge, and it has since been changed again to the Inn at Thorn Hill. It continues to be known for its fine dining, excellent service, and art workshops.

The Panorama Slope of the Thorn Mountain Ski Area was accessed off of Thorn Hill Road. The ski area flourished in the 1940s and '50s. Both the Thorn Mountain and Black Mountain Ski Areas were linked by the Jackson cross country ski trails.

The Thorn Mountain Ski Area covered 1,200 acres, and had a 4,000-foot chair lift, a verticle rise of 1,110 feet, 2 restaurants, 3 warming huts, a ski repair shop, 2 rope tows, and a ski school with Rink Earle as director.

Gray's Inn and Iron Mountain can be seen in the background of this photograph of the Thorn Mountain Ski Area taken from the top of Hog Back.

Thorn Mountain Cabin.   JACKSON, N. H.

This postcard, dated July 9, 1918, is of the Thorn Mountain Cabin and was sent by a Miss Virginia Adams, who wrote about the eight wonderful weeks she spent in the White Mountains. The cabin later served as a private camp of the Bushee family.

This interior view of the cabin shows the large fireplace, bunk beds, loft, rifles, tools, and furnishings of the early settlers.

This is a view from The Poplars, originally known as Gray's Farm and later called Thorn Hill Cottage in the late 1890s. Mrs. Bradbury Bedell acquired the property in 1904.

Mrs. Bedell, upon overhearing the comment from a sightseeing stage driver that "the widder lady lives in that house," promptly had the road moved to allow her a greater degree of privacy.

This photograph offers a majestic view of Mount Washington from Thorn Mountain. Note the large areas of cleared land in the outskirts of the village.

A view of the road that comes up the backside of Thorn Hill from the village of Intervale. The old Pitman farm sits to the left in this photograph.

Jackson from Thorn Mt. Park.

A view from Thorn Mountain Park overlooking Jackson, with Gray's Inn and the Wentworth Hall clearly visible in the background.

Note the ice cone to the left of Gray's Inn in this February 28, 1928, postcard, with Iron Mountain serving as a backdrop on this cold winter day.

The Gray's Inn herd grazing at the Thorn Mountain Park in the early 1900s. Most of the larger inns had their own farms to supply fresh produce, milk, cream, and butter to their guests.

This George Slade photograph from August 1905 captures the beauty of the many white birch trees that once reigned in the forests of Jackson.

Many natural rock formations resemble famous people, as in this photograph of Jackson's own Washington Boulder, or Profile. The boulder resides in Thorn Mountain Park on the road to the old Tyrol Ski Area. The park and rock were popular tourist attractions in the early 1900s. It is rumored that local photographer A.E. Phinney discovered a Ben Franklin profile rock, but no additional information on the location of this "find" is available.

View from **Tyrol** -at-Jackson, New Hampshire
Vacation Chalet Village

Tyrol's unparalleled view of the Huntington and Presidential Mountain Ranges. Tyrol combined true alpine living with the convenience of town roads, electricity, and telephones. Its pool and ski facilities further enhanced the charm of having your own four season chalet or vacation home (or so this postcard of the new Tyrol development claimed). Today, only the homes remain.

Snow can still be seen lingering on the Presidential Range in mid-July when this photograph was taken from Jackson.

Four
Black Mountain

Once known as Perkins Cottages (now the Christmas Farm Inn), this small cape unit was the original home of Rufus Pinkham (son of Joseph Pinkham, one of the first settlers). After Chase B. Perkins purchased the home from his brother Pike, he began taking on boarders.

While Perkins owned the property, the abandoned Free-Will Baptist Church was moved by oxen and rollers from its triangle location and attached to the cape building extension. It is said that the cape building once served as the town jail.

The property was purchased in 1941 as a Christmas present to a Philadelphia man's daughter. She immediately changed the name to Christmas Farm. In 1946 Richard Welch purchased the property and added Inn to the Christmas Farm name. The name remains today, and the inn is owned and operated by the Zeliff family.

In the late 1800s the Wilsons, who owned this home just beyond the Great Brook on what is now Wilson Road, began taking in summer boarders. Frank and Laura Proctor Wilson sold the property in 1904 to Mark Proctor. Today the building is being used as a private residence.

With the growth of business, additional buildings were added in the early 1900s. The Wilson Cottages became so successful that tents were used on neighbor's lawns to accommodate guests. For $18 a week you received three (all you could eat) meals a day and the use of the tennis courts, swimming pool, nightly dances, and quiet parlors.

The Davis cows are on their way home after grazing on Black Mountain. Noah Davis, one of the first settlers in Jackson, built a farm just south of this location. In the years that followed, Dean and Eva Davis took in boarders year-round. Today the farm homestead remains in use as the private residence of their grandson Dean R. Davis.

This was known as the George Hackett Homestead Farm when it was purchased by Edwin Moody in 1894. The Hackett's tradition of taking in boarders was continued by the Moodys, who soon added on to accommodate the increasing number of tourists. Four cabins were built along the Great Brook and a dance hall was also constructed.

In the early 1930s skiers flocked to the hill behind Moody's and stayed in the boarding house for $2 per day (which included three meals). In the winter of 1935 Ed Moody, George Morton, and Phil Robertson invented, supplied, and promoted the first overhead cable ski lift in the country.

When Bill and Betty Whitney purchased the Moody place in 1936, they renamed it Whitneys' in Jackson. Their specific interest was skiing, and in 1937 they ordered a number of shovel handles from Sears, Roebuck & Company and redesigned the lift using the handles to make it easier to ride. This bit of Yankee ingenuity remained until finally replaced in 1949.

Whitneys' in Jackson was closed during the war, but shortly after Halsey Davis, Stanton Davis, and Bill Whitney formed the Black Mountain Tramways Corporation and additional land was purchased and leased from Dean Davis for ninety-nine years of skiing.

WHITNEYS' in JACKSON WHITNEYS' in JACKSON

Winter Tariff: 1940-41

In the Inn:	Day	Week
Rooms with running water	$4.00	$26.00
Other rooms	3.75	25.00
There are several large rooms that will accommodate three or four comfortably and when used this way, the rate is	3.50	23.00
The rate is increased 10% if a double room is used by only one person.		
In the Lodge	3.25	21.50

Phone, write or wire

WHITNEYS' IN JACKSON, N. H.

Bill & Betty Whitney, *hosts*

Restricted Clientele

This 1940–41 brochure informed visitors that Whitneys' in Jackson was definitely the ideal place for winter vacations and had everything you could need right at the door. It offered miles of trails and slopes surrounding the comfortable, homey inn and adjoining lodge, and the dining room overlooked the main hill and tramway, where the Eastern Slope Ski School held many of its classes.

JUST TO REMIND YOU

WHITNEYS' in JACKSON

SUMMER SEASON

SERVING

Weekdays	Lunch	12:30 - 1:30	$1.50
	Dinner	6:30 - 7:30	$2.00
Sundays	Dinner	12:30 - 2:00	$2.00
	Smorgasbord Supper	6:30 - 7:30	$1.50

▶ Special menus for special occasions at special times by reservation ◀

This 1953 postcard reminds the local residents and past guests of Whitneys' summer season weekday and Sunday dining hours and rates. The $1.50 Sunday Smorgasbord Supper must have been a favorite for all.

The Brookside Shop was one of the cottages built to accommodate the overflow of guests. Over the years it has also served as a gift shop, as can be seen in this photograph.

A view of Black Mountain and the proposed site of the chair lift to be built in the summer of 1948. A Roebling T-Bar lift 3,500 feet in length was installed. Black Mountain Tramways was then a ski area of 1,000 acres, with a vertical rise of 750 feet, a canteen, warming huts on the slopes, and a ski school with Arthur Doucette as director.

Trails with the names of Sugarbush, Black Beauty, Spruce Run, Juniper, Galloping Goose, Runaway, Jackson Standard, Maple Slalom, Black Diamond, Roller Coaster, Big Dipper, Speedwell, Bob-O-Link, Jubilee, and Davis were available to the early skiers.

After a hard day on the slopes, the many skiers at Whitneys' in Jackson relaxed by playing cards, board games, reading in the library, or carrying on discussions that were certain to solve the problems of the world.

Skiing was fun at Black Mountain, with hundreds of acres of extra wide slopes for beginners as well as challenging trails for any potential Olympic skiers in the family.

A BMT Patrol member heads out to groom the trails. Extensive snow farming and grooming equipment operated all night if need be to keep snow properly packed. And the snow-making machinery on the J-Bar area was a further guarantee of good skiing throughout the winter.

Black Mountain, set among the majestic mountains of the Presidential Range, is in the heart of Mount Washington Valley. Just three hours from Boston, four hours from Hartford, and seven hours from New York, area roads were plowed and sanded all winter to allow easy access. According to an old Black Mountain brochure, you could plan a five day "ski week," a weekend, or whole vacation around superb skiing and fine accommodations. It was sure to be an experience that you and your family would long remember.

BLACK MOUNTAIN SKI LIFT RATES
Saturdays, Sundays and Holiday Weeks

	ALL LIFTS		BAR LIFTS		J-BAR only	
	Adults	Juniors	Adults	Juniors	Adults	Juniors
All Day	$7.00	$5.50	$6.00	$4.50	$5.00	$3.50
½ Day (P.M.)	5.00	4.00	4.50	3.50	3.50	2.50
Weekdays						
All Day	5.00	4.00	—	—	4.00	3.00
½ Day (P.M.)	4.00	3.50	—	—	2.50	2.00

SEASON FAMILY PLAN — ALL LIFTS
First member of a family $125.00
Second member 95.00
Each additional member 50.00
A 10% discount is allowed if purchased before November 15

BLACK MOUNTAIN PACKAGE PLAN
5 Full days' use of lifts plus four, two-hour Ski School lessons at Black.

PRICE: $25.00 Adult
$20.00 Junior

Available to Whitneys' guests only
Holiday weeks excepted.

INTERCHANGEABLE PACKAGE PLAN

PLAN A   BIG HOLIDAY TICKET — 5 day — 5 way ticket for lifts and ten ski school lessons at Black, Cranmore, Wildcat, Attitash and Tyrol Mountains, Monday through Friday.

PRICE: $45.00

Note: The above plan is available only thru participating inn members of the Mount Washington Valley. Holiday weeks excepted. Ideal accommodations available at Whitneys' Inn right at the base of Black Mt.

PLAN B   5 consecutive days — 5-way lift ticket for lifts at Black, Cranmore, Wildcat, Attitash and Tyrol Mountains.

PRICE: $30.00

PLAN C $50.00 Coupon Book for lifts or lessons at Black, Cranmore, Wildcat, Attitash and Tyrol Mountains.

PRICE: $45.00

SKI SCHOOL
Black Mt. Ski School under the direction of "Sonny" Lynch conducts lessons daily, with extra beginners lessons on weekends and holidays. Special classes conducted weekly, including a Mt. Training Class every Sunday during the season. "Sonny" is USEASA certified and a charter member of PSIA. He has a staff of competent assistants working with him.

Ski School Rates
Half Day Lesson . . . . $ 5.00
Full Day Lesson 9.00
Eight Lesson Book 28.00
Forty Lesson Book 120.00
Group rates on request.

Daytime (603) 383-4490
Nights or off season (603) 383-4291

BLACK MOUNTAIN
ski area

skiing
in
the
heart
of
Mt.
Washington
valley

Jackson, New Hampshire 03846

This is a copy of a Black Mountain Ski Area brochure from the 1950s offering its interchangeable package plan, including the ski areas of Black, Cranmore, Attitash, Wildcat, and Tyrol Mountains. Prices were included, with an interior map of facilities, lifts, and trails, as well as lodging information at nearby Whitneys' in Jackson.

This photograph from a Black Mountain Ski Area chair lift gives us a fantastic view, minus the snow and cold weather. The lovely lady seems to be enjoying the beauty of the surrounding White Mountains.

A view of Black Mountain, with its elevation of 2,758 feet. Its trails are clearly visible, and even in the summer months it beckons visitors the moment they come through the Jackson Covered Bridge.

The Appalachian Mountain Club fire tower which sat on Black Mountain for many years was used to watch the surrounding national forests for forest fires in the dry seasons of the year.

With Black Mountain to the immediate right, this photograph was taken coming down Dundee Road toward the village. The Presidential Range encompasses the entire background of this photograph.

Brookbank, on the Five Mile Circuit Road just up from Moody's Farm, was purchased by Ed and Ada Moody in 1936. It was used, along with three cabins, to take in boarders until the 1940s, and is now a private residence owned by Bob Cheney.

Back tracking a bit, we travel down Wilson Road for this view of Birchbank, now a private residence, that sits near the Great Brook in the area once known as the "triangle."

In 1903 Arthur Howe purchased the Wilson Farm, now called the Overlook, and came with his four children in 1904 for the summer months. The original part of the house was built in the early 1840s. Additions were made over the years and family, friends, and friends of friends were often found visiting during the spring and summer months. In the late 1930s Stanley Howe opened the house to skiers.

Overlook closed during World War II but reopened in 1946 as a communal adventure of six families and their small children. Today, it remains in the Howe family and serves as a private residence.

The old Burgess place sits in the background of this photograph, as the road curves to the right and heads west toward the Carter Notch Road.

This early view of the Presidential Range from the Five Mile Circuit Road shows open fields that have most likely now been reclaimed by trees and brush.

Five

Jackson Falls
and Carter Notch

The Crow's Nest at the base of the Jackson Falls in 1915 was a favorite spot for romance, long lunches, or just to watch the Wildcat River flow by.

Looking downstream in February 1925 from the Crow's Nest, we can see the Stone Bridge has not yet been constructed. Upon its completion, the Iron Bridge was moved upstream to Valley Cross Road.

This is a 1937 postcard of the Wentworth Hall Solarium, located on the Wildcat River below Jackson Falls. The swimming pool was just below the Solarium, and had steps descending to it.

The swimming pool of the Wentworth Hall, below the Solarium, served the resort well for many years. Every fall the Solarium was dismantled and then reassembled the following summer. There were many times over the years, after a downpour, that parts would wash away with the rapid and surging waters from the Jackson Falls. Many of the original pilings and foundations can still be seen amid the lower falls.

Two of the entertainers as they perform their antics in the Wentworth swimming pool. The Wentworth Hall management was constantly bringing in different acts to entertain and amuse the vacationing guests.

Three lucky guests of the Wentworth enjoy the famous—and only one of its kind—electric spray showers after a dip in the Wildcat River.

The Solarium, as Wentworth Hall, was always alive with the music of big name entertainers and bands traveling from Boston, Portland, and New York. On this warm summer evening, suit coats and formal dresses have replaced the Victorian wear of the previous photographs, as the Wentworth Hall continues to appeal to the wealthy upper class of vacationers.

Lunch on the pool deck in this early postcard shows a change in style from the previous page, but proper dress still prevails in an air of refinement.

A more casual lunch on the pool deck, as modern square cut lumber railings have replaced the rustic shaped logs in the top photograph.

Wednesday, August 7, 1968

LUNCH

APPETIZERS . . .
Chilled Pineapple Juice   Fruit Cup   Melon in Season
Sliced Egg with Russian Dressing

SOUPS . . .
Cream of Asparagus   Cold Red Beet Borscht, Sour Cream

ENTREES . . .
Golden Brown Omelette with Mushrooms
Fried Long Island Scallops, Tartar Sauce
Stuffed Cabbage a la Hongroise en Casserole
Braised Short Ribs of Beef, Jardiniere
Fresh Garden Vegetable Dinner, Poached Egg

VEGETABLES . . .
Mixed Vegetables   Mashed Potatoes   Parsley Potato

COLD BUFFET . . .
Bowl of Sour Cream with Bananas
Chef's Salad Bowl, Julienne of Turkey, Tongue and Swiss Cheese
Bumble Bee Tunafish Salad on Crisp Lettuce

DESSERTS . . .
Maple Walnut Layer Cake   Montmorency Cherry Pie
Lemon Danish Pastry   Assorted Butter Cookies   Chocolate Sundae
Jello, Whipped Cream   Orange or Raspberry Sherbet
Coffee, Chocolate or Vanilla Ice Cream
Cheeses: Camembert   Bleu   Swiss Gruyere

BEVERAGES . . .
Coffee   Tea   Milk   Postum   Buttermilk
Iced Coffee   Sanka   Iced Tea

A lunch menu for Wentworth hall guests from 1968. It looks like a delightful way to spend the afternoon—Cold Red Beet Borscht, followed by Stuffed Cabbage a la Horngrise en Casserole, with Montmorency Cherry Pie for dessert—then a dip in the pool. Note that Bumble Bee Tunafish is the brand of choice of the Wentworth chefs.

This is a view of the village from the Wentworth Castle. Most of the buildings in this photograph are part of the Wentworth Hall complex, with the exception of the Jackson Community Church and Gray's Inn (in the background).

This is the Wentworth Castle, built as a private residence by General Marshall Wentworth for his wife. Located to the west of the Jackson Falls, the Castle has continued to be used as a private residence throughout the years, once by a Countess, and has undergone renovations by its numerous owners. Its exterior appearance, however, remains the same today as it did in this 1907 photograph.

George Slade, a local Jackson photographer, took this postcard view of the Jackson Falls Park. It is a great place to explore, enjoy the upper falls, and sun yourself on the rocks.

In this September 1921 photograph, we can see the upper falls and the Fairview Bridge (in the background), from which Valley Cross Road connects the Black Mountain and Carter Notch Roads.

An early water wheel on the Wildcat River at the Jackson Falls. The Wentworth Hall complex once had its own electric plant on the river to generate power for its many buildings.

This postcard produced for Howard Robinson's store, the Wigwam, is of the water wheel on the Jackson Falls. Some of the tubing used to direct and harness the water supply is still evident and easily viewed when the river is low.

A view of the Fairview Bridge, spanning the river at the top of the Jackson Falls. This bridge was replaced with the Iron Bridge in the 1930s when the new Stone Bridge was constructed near the church.

On this postcard dated March 1939, "B" writes, "This is what Jackson looks like right now—20 inches of soft snow and it's wonderful for snowshoeing. Wire or phone if you can come (Jackson, 23 ring 12) and you'll be met at the Intervale station—lots of room here—a swell place and good food."

The Jackson Falls drop gradually over a half mile, a total of 150 feet, and have been a focal point for visitors and residents alike. It continues to be one of the first sites that visitors are suggested to view, and after a rain storm the din from the falls is deafening.

From the top of Jackson Falls, we look out over the village viewing Gray's Inn in the background of this foreboding photograph.

As Carter Notch Road winds its way past Jackson Falls and out of the village, we come across Lover's Lane, so titled in this 1911 photograph taken by George Slade.

Above the Jackson Falls, the Wildcat River (now classified as a federally protected wild and scenic river) winds lazily north to its beginnings in the mighty Presidential Range of the White Mountains.

Just south of the Eagle Mountain House on the golf course sits a gazebo, very similar to this summer house of September 1903. Remember when the mail was stamped with the time of cancellation? This card was stamped at 5 am on September 9, 1903, in Jackson.

Carter Notch and the Wildcat River are the only company that these two farm animals, belonging to the Eagle Mountain House farm, have on this warm summer day.

The eighth fairway of the 9-hole Eagle Mountain Golf Course on the Wildcat River, which served as a natural hazard and proud collector of many golf balls over the years. The course was originally 6 holes and opened in 1900.

This swimming pool at the Eagle Mountain House, better known as Gale's Pond, was used and enjoyed by many of the children of Jackson, as well as visitors from throughout New England. There are many current residents who speak fondly of learning how to swim at Gale's Pond.

Cyrus and Marcia (maiden name of Pinkham) Gale opened the original Eagle Mountain House in 1879. From twelve guests, it grew in time to have a capacity of 125 people, and was open in the winter for parties, snowshoeing, sliding, and skiing on the slopes and trails surrounding the hotel. It burned down in 1915.

Eagle Hall was erected in 1890 and connected to the main house by a covered walk. A 32-by-45-foot dancing hall was located inside, along with a billiard room, a card room, and a cloak room. The hall was heated by very large open fireplaces and the corridors above by a hot water system.

The Eglet was constructed to accommodate additional guests and was also used to house the staff of the Eagle Mountain House. Carter Dome and Carter Notch are visible from the piazza and pure spring water flows from the side of Eagle Mountain.

"Pa" and "Ma," as they were known to visiting guests, staff, and residents of the village, were Cyrus and Marcia Gale. They built and operated the Eagle Mountain House from 1879 until the mid-1910s when their son, Arthur P. Gale, acquired the property.

OFFICE EAGLE MOUNTAIN HOUSE
JACKSON. N. H.
NO. 251

The interior of the Eagle Mountain House prior to the devastating fire of 1915. The house was situated on the east side of Eagle Mountain, 1,100 feet above sea level, 300 feet above the village of Jackson, and within 100 rods of the famous Jackson Falls. It opened June 1 for trout fishing, and afforded many rare views for lovers of the sport. A brochure from the early 1900s claimed that a fine trout stream with shady banks was within 50 rods, and that the stream wound through a beautiful intervale dotted with magnificent elms and surrounded by mountains. According to the brochure, ten of the mountains could be seen from the piazza of the Eagle Mountain House.

The Eagle Mountain House had its own 6-hole (later expanded to a 9-hole) golf course laid out by Stewart; a beautiful bathing pond, with bath houses for both ladies and gentleman; its own three-piece orchestra; grass and dirt tennis courts; and croquet grounds. Lovers of duplicate whist were encouraged to visit.

The Eagle Mountain House in 1900 claimed to be three hours from Portland, five hours from Boston, and twelve hours from New York. You could buy tickets to Glen station on the Maine Central Railroad, and then take the Eagle Mountain carriage to the house, a distance of 4 miles.

Arthur P. Gale, son of Cyrus and Marcia, continued to operate the house until his death in 1957. His sister, Marcia Chadborne, and her husband Orin operated the house until 1973. For years, the house maintained its own dairy, vegetable gardens, golf course, spacious lawns and flower beds, tennis courts, two putting greens, swimming pool and pond, and orchestra. The Eagle Mountain House was only one of two hotels in Jackson to have its own elevator.

The dining room illustrates the capacity of the Eagle Mountain House, with all of the dairy products, fresh produce, and flowers being supplied by its own staff and farm.

A flock of Eagle Mountain House sheep grazing in one of the fields adjacent to the 6-hole golf course along the Wildcat River.

In 1816 Spencer Wentworth settled on Spruce Mountain, and he and his son Warren raised sheep and tended to a farm on the 170 acres. In 1911 Warren's son, Winfield, sold the property to Mable Slade of Providence, Rhode Island. Mable and her partner, Lilla Belle Colburn, built up a tourist business by renting tented platforms to visitors, and thus established the Spruce Mountain Bungalow Camps. The first cottages were made of canvas and they continued to construct separate buildings to supplement the main lodge. The Spruce Mountain Lodge was one of the most popular spots in Jackson, and the first rope tow was built behind the lodge.

The following description of the Spruce Mountain Camps is from an old brochure: "The bungalows are attractively arranged within a short distance of the main Lodge. Each bungalow has running hot and cold water, toilet, lavatory, shower bath, hardwood floors, open fireplace, electricity, comfy chairs, and piazza. Persons affected with tuberculosis are not permitted in the Camp."

The Spruce Mountain Lodge was sold in 1944 to the Klinquists. It was then owned by the Mallards and the Barnes, and in 1976 it was sold to Rodriguez, McGuire, Tardiff, and Zablicki. It is currently owned privately, with some of the cabins rented to local residents. Mable Slade, better known as "Auntie Mae," died in 1971 at the age of eighty-five.

This spot along the Wildcat River could very well be where guests of the Spruce Mountain Lodge traveled to swim in the cold, clear pools.

Taken just north of the Eagle Mountain House, this photograph shows Carter Notch as clouds are about to roll overhead.

The old Cyrus Perkins farm on Carter Notch Road became a boarding house in 1916 after it was sold to Sylvester and Zella Mae Robinson. The Cliff Cottage claimed to be 1,200 feet above sea level and in the heart of the White Mountains. It was located near the banks of the Wildcat River, and the Black, Thorn, Moat, Carter Dome, Spruce, and Cliff Mountains are all visible from the property. Shade trees, tennis courts, croquet, and pure water from mountain springs were always available.

The Cliff Cottage continued until 1926 when it was sold to Alden Stevens. In 1930 it was sold again, to the Robinsons of Boston. Between 1930 and 1950 it was operated as Thor's Lodge, and Thor's Restaurant was a favorite of visitors and residents of the village.

In 1950 members of the Drifter's Ski Club, a group of Harvard graduates, purchased the property. It is still owned by the club today, and members from all over New England use it for family vacations and ski weekends.

Fernald Cottages, located on Carter Notch Road, faced Black Mountain with Carter Notch and Wildcat Mountain to the north, and was originally the John Patrick Farm. The Osbourne Freeman Fernalds bought the farm in 1890, and in 1892 they housed eight boarders who were working nearby. Evelyn Fernald Nutter and her husband ran Fernald Cottages after the death of Osbourne in 1940.

This postcard shows the Fernald Cottages dining room. The cottages claimed to be a cozy farm home overlooking Carter Notch Valley and the surrounding mountains. Modern conveniences, reasonable rates, and home-cooked food were the major selling points.

Carter Notch can be seen in the background as these residents of the village and their guests enjoy a pleasant afternoon of sightseeing.

The same location in February 1921. The darkness of winter has descended upon the Carter Notch Valley and only skiers and snowshoers dare to venture out.

Logging operations continue today in and around the village of Jackson, with much of it being done in the Carter Notch area. Being surrounded by National Forest, it is evident that the early settlers did a great deal of clear cutting. In 1850 New Hampshire claimed less then half of its total acreage as uncleared land. The forests in and around Jackson were the primary source of material for the clothes pin factory, the dowel factory, and the sawmill once located near Mill Pond.

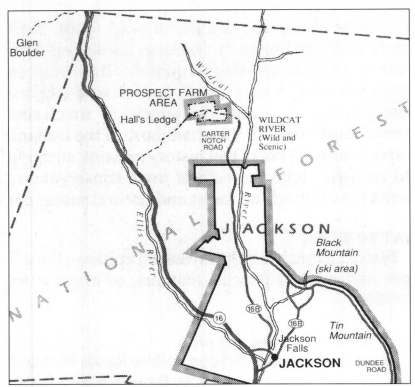

This map indicates the location of Prospect Farm, beyond the end of Carter Notch Road. In 1942 Edith C. Baker willed the land, known as Prospect Farm, to the town of Jackson. This map is from the guide produced by the Tin Mountain Conservation Center entitled *Fragments That Remain* (1989).

This is a photograph of the Charles and Edith Baker farm, on the property known as Prospect Farm, north of Jackson in the midst of the White Mountain National Forest. Only fragments remain of the foundation of this old farm, which housed some of Jackson's first settlers.